Published by H2 Publishing
www.drlisahoover.com

ISBN: 979-8-9993903-4-9
Printed in the United States of America

Welcome!

You don't have to love numbers to respect them.
Around here, we use them like tools—not rulers.
This journal is where your clarity will start telling the
truth out loud: what you value, what you're willing to
change, and what you'll build next.

Take your time. Tell the truth. Then move.

How to Use This Journal:
- Write freely, without judgment.
- Use it daily, weekly, or whenever you need a reset.
- Revisit your answers often—your clarity will grow
  with each page.

*"It was never just about the numbers — it was about the
story they tell."*

SECTION ONE: CLARITY & PURPOSE

Section 1: Clarity & Purpose

- What does living on purpose mean to me?
- Where in my life do I feel most aligned with my values?

One dream I've been afraid to speak out loud is…

Clarity & Purpose

Clarity & Purpose

Clarity & Purpose

Clarity & Purpose

Clarity & Purpose

SECTION TWO: NUMBERS THAT MATTER

Section 2: Numbers That Matter

List 3 numbers that currently define my life (credit, income, debt, goals, etc.): 1. 2. 3.

Which of these numbers truly reflect who I am? Which do I want to change — and why?

"Numbers are powerful—but they don't define you."

Numbers That Matter

Numbers That Matter

Numbers That Matter

Numbers That Matter

Numbers That Matter

SECTION THREE: STRATEGY & GOALS

Section 3: Strategy & Goals

One goal I will achieve in the next 30 days is…
Steps I can take this week toward that goal: 1.
2. 3.

What obstacles might come up?

How will I face them?

"Legacy isn't what we leave behind—it's what we build while we're here."

Straegy & Goals

Straegy & Goals

Straegy & Goals

Straegy & Goals

Straegy & Goals

SECTION FOUR: MY 2 CENTS REFLECTIONS

Section 4: My 2 Cents

Today I learned…
The hardest truth I've faced about my finances is…
A small win I want to celebrate is…

If I could give advice to myself 10 years ago, it would be…

"My 2 Cents: Reflection turns information into transformation."

My 2 Cents

My 2 Cents

My 2 Cents

My 2 Cents

My 2 Cents

My 2 Cents

SECTION FIVE: LEGACY & IMPACT

Section 5: Legacy & Impact

Who am I building this for besides myself?
What story do I want my children, family, or
community to tell about me?
How do I want my numbers to reflect my legacy?

*"Legacy isn't what we leave behind—it's what we build
while we're here."*

Legacy & Impact

Legacy & Impact

Legacy & Impact

Legacy & Impact

WEEKLY TRACKER

Weekly Tracker

This Week My Focus Number Is:

Actions I Took:

Wins:
Lessons:

Weekly Tracker

Weekly Tracker

This Week My Focus Number Is:

Actions I Took:

Wins:
Lessons:

Weekly Tracker

Weekly Tracker

This Week My Focus Number Is:

Actions I Took:

Wins:
Lessons:

Weekly Tracker

Weekly Tracker

This Week My Focus Number Is:

Actions I Took:

Wins:
Lessons:

Weekly Tracker — Focus / Actions / Wins / Lessons

Weekly Tracker

CLOSING REFLECTION

"It was never just about the numbers — it was about the story they tell.
And I get to choose what story mine will tell moving forward."

Use this page as your final reflection after completing the journal.

Signed, ________________________
Date: ________________________

ABOUT THE AUTHOR

Dr. Lisa Hoover

Educator | Realtor | Coach | Advocate

Dr.Lisa Hoover believesevery opportunityis
either a win or a learn.
Through her books, coaching, and educational
programs, she helps people rewrite their financial
and personal narratives with clarity, confidence,
and purpose.

www.drlisahoover.com
@LevelUpwithDrLisaHoover
lisa@drlisahoover.com

www.ingramcontent.com/pod-product-compliance
Lightning Source LLC
Chambersburg PA
CBHW041836110726
48006CB00020B/2650